IN LOVING MEMORY OF MY DAUGHTER

DESIREE MARLISE

To my son, Rudy, and my daughter, Colleen – much love and thanks…

For without them, I would not be writing this book. They have kept me grounded and reminded me that I had a lot to live for.

To my life partner and husband, Robert, for standing by me, loving me, and accepting me as I am.

COPYRIGHT © 2014 by Nancy Hite

All Rights Reserved.

ISNB: 978-0-9977096-1-2

First Edition: July 2017
Published by: Nancy Hite
Editor: Amber Lennon
Illustrations, Photographs, Cover and Book Design by: Rudy Loupias
Social Media: Colleen Vizents
Printed in the United States of America
ALL RIGHTS RESERVED. NO PART OF THIS BOOK MAY BE USED OR REPRODUCED IN ANY MANNER WHATSOEVER WITHOUT WRITTEN PERMISSION, EXCEPT IN THE CASE OF BRIEF QUOTATIONS EMBODIED IN CRITICAL ARTICLES OR REVIEWS. FOR INFORMATION CONTACT:
Library of Congress, Copyright Office, Public Information Office 101 Independence Ave SE, Washington, DC 20559-6000

arrangement

Author's Note:

Everything I have written in this book is from my own experiences as I lived them, and also from the relationships with other parents, as they too lived through the trials and hard-fought battles with their child's Cystic Fibrosis.

If I can help even one person get through life after hearing that their child has a life-threatening disease or an accident that changes their life forever, then it will be worth every second spent working on this book. Much of the proceeds from this book will be donated to Make-A-Wish, Ronald McDonald House, and the CF Foundation to help make life a little easier for children and their families.

"God grant me the serenity to accept the things that I cannot change, the courage to change the things that I can, and the wisdom to know the difference."

~Reinhold Niebuhr

Chapter 1

Getting the News:

- ***Your first reaction*** - absolute SHOCK & disbelief, then the heartache.

- ***Talking to your child.***

    How do you tell your child they are very sick or may not completely recover from their accident? When your child asks questions about their condition, tell them the truth as much as possible without scaring them; get good advice from their doctor or therapist.

- ***Do your research.***

    What's next? Get as much information as you can. If you do not have a computer at home, you can use the computers in your local library, or many hospitals have computers and/or libraries that the patient's family may use.

- ***Write your questions down.***

    I know there are thousands of questions running around in your head - write them down as you think of them, and ask your child's doctor or social worker at the hospital. Ask for information about your child's disease/condition. What kinds of treatments are available? How long will the treatments last? Will my child ever be back to normal? Will I be able to manage my child's needs at home? Can I get help? And one more thing - bring someone with you that is not as emotionally involved in this situation to make notes on important information the doctors and others will give you. Remembering everything during this stressful time is impossible.

Chapter 2

Managing Big Changes:

- ***Your life is going to change***, A LOT, and it may never be the same again.

- ***Find a good therapist or support group.***

    Many times, this change in your life can put a deep, unrecoverable strain on a marriage or partnership. Get help from a professional to answer questions and support you. You are going to need it through your whole journey.

- ***Remember - It is not your fault.***

    Do not listen to anyone who tells you that you are at fault for your child's sickness, when it is, in fact, a defect or disease that they were born with. When life starts at conception, things we have no control over do happen.

    For those whose children were involved in a horrible accident or victim of a crime, taking on self-blame is common. As parents we cannot be everywhere at all times. Unfortunately, horrible things happen regardless of age, race, how much money we make, how careful we think we have been, or the education we have given them.

- ***Do not forget your other children or partner if you have them.***

    Ask them how they want to be involved, share your feelings, and let your child/partner share their feelings with you and their siblings. Seek professional help to support them, if needed.

- **Tell your child how much you love them every chance you get.**

"The truth is, you do not know what is going to happen tomorrow. Life is a crazy ride and nothing is guaranteed."

~Eminem

Chapter 3

Rearranging Your Life – Time to Get Organized:

Wow, you thought life was already stressful, now it is complete insanity!

- Think about what exactly will be needed:

    1. Doctor or treatment appointments?
    2. What treatments and how long will it take?
    3. Hospitalizations - can you expect a lot of them?
    4. Will you need to make arrangements for schedules at home? Getting your other children to school, daycare, or after school activities? Reach out to your support network, and get help arranged for when you need it. Maybe grandparents, friends, members of church or social groups.
    5. How much time will you need to take off from work to do all of this? Doctor appointments, treatment days or staying at the hospital with them - just during the day or overnight?

6. Apply for medical coverage if needed. Medical Social Workers at the hospital can help with this. Medicaid can be a very good secondary insurance if you have low income and also have health insurance with your employer.
7. Are you going to need alterations in the home, such as a ramp for wheelchair, or setting up a bedroom downstairs near a bathroom?
8. Ask what medical equipment you may need for home and how to order it. The hospital staff usually will take care of this before the child is sent home.
9. Take time to BREATHE. Find what helps you function, like praying or meditation, talking to a close friend.
10. Try to laugh every chance you get, and dance if you can. I know you feel that you cannot do that. Why would you laugh or dance during this horrible time in your life? It really helps you survive another day, lifts your mood, and keeps you going. Like any other job, you need to take a break once in a while.

"The best way to mend a broken heart is time and girlfriends."

~Gwyneth Paltrow

Chapter 4

When Care at Home Fails

As much as you would like to think you could do it all, caring for an acutely ill or disabled child is extremely difficult, even with help. It can be rewarding to know that your child is getting personal care that may not be available at home. You feel that you can do things better because you know your child, right?

Well, there are times when you must give yourself a break. There are services that allow you to get much needed respite care for your child.

What is "respite care"?

Respite care is temporary institutional care for a dependent child or adult who is ill or handicapped. In other words, your child stays in a nursing home where specialized staff members can care for your child around the clock, in order to provide relief for their usual caregivers. You get much needed rest, both mentally & physically. Spend time with your family, or take a short vacation.

I know you are saying, "I can't do that!" Well you really must do that, because if you don't, you are going to burn out, and you may become very ill yourself! There's only so much a human body can take. And if you get sick, you can infect your ill child, the family can get sick, or the flu bug can put you in the hospital, and then who takes your place? You get the picture.

In Washington State, there is a program that provides private duty nursing in the home, known as the Medically Intensive Children's Program. Once approved for these services, private duty nurses can provide full care up to 16 hours a day. If caring for your child at home is not possible at all (for many different reasons), there are several options available, and I have listed these in the resource section at the end of this guide.

"Your job as a parent is to give your kids not only the instincts and talent to survive, but to help them enjoy their lives."

~Susan Sarandon

Chapter 5

No Regrets

I know that you want to keep your child wrapped up in a blanket of protection and let nothing else happen to them, but it's important to allow your child to do as many things as they possibly can to feel normal. They still want to be like their friends.

Many children go to specialized summer camps, which are suited for the type of illness or disability they have. These camps have the medical providers, medical supplies, counselors and special equipment that the kids would need during their stay at camp.

The kids come home feeling so special. They make friends with other children that are just like them, so they do not feel so all alone in their journey. You can ask the counselors at the hospital or look these camps up on the internet for more information. They are usually no cost to the families.

Why do I tell you this?

Because when the time comes and they are no longer with us, you will not have any regrets knowing your child lived life to the fullest. Believe me, you may have this running thought later, *why did I do that*? Or, *I wish I had done more.* It only adds a lot more to your grief, so allow your child as much freedom as is safely possible. I know it is hard, but push your child to do all they can. My daughter - even though I was scared to death - went to college for a year and stayed in a college dorm room with everyone else. Yes, she got sick several times, but the risk was worth the experience she had.

"When we meet real tragedy in life, we can react in two ways: either by losing hope and falling into self-destructive habits, or by using the challenge to find our inner strength."

~Author Unknown

Chapter 6

When the time comes, the end of life...STOP & BREATHE

For me, I could not believe what had just happened, my child had just passed away, and everyone was still going about their lives as if nothing had happened!

I felt like I was somewhere else, somewhere out in space, not really here. I wanted to scream at the top of my lungs, *Stop the world, I am getting off.* The last place I wanted to be was here on this planet.

All of a sudden, like a lightning bolt, absolutely nothing was the same, nothing mattered. *I do not want to be here!*

This is one of the most difficult times of your life, knowing that your child will not be coming home. Their room and all their belongings smell like them. You look at all of the things they used, touched, wore, and slept in, and you go into a meltdown of grief. It is the hardest thing in the world to clean out their room and give away their belongings. Depending on your situation, do not do anything until you are really ready.

Give yourself time. **BREATHE**.

Choose a couple of special items to keep that will always bring back good memories. These memories will keep your child close to you, and they will smile with you.

My own personal belief is that there is no such thing as death - we just do not keep the shell (physical body) we live in here. We are spiritual beings having an earthly experience. You may not believe in any Supreme Source of life at all, and that is fine. You have your own beliefs and may find peace in the beautiful memories and life of the child that was created.

Note: I must mention the possibility of being approached by hospital staff about donating your child's organs. Many parents just cannot deal with this question in such an emotional state. Ask how much time you have to decide because you need to make an informed decision. Some parents that have decided to donate their child's organs went on to meet the recipient of the organ and had such a sense of joy knowing that a part of their child lives, and the joy from the recipient / recipient's family can be so healing.

Certain religious faiths forbid organ donation, and this sometimes just takes the decision out of your hands.

*"They shall grow not old, as we that are left grow old.
Age shall not weary them, nor the years condemn,
At the going down of the sun and in the morning we will remember them."*

~Author Unknown

Chapter 7

Planning a Celebration of Life

When you are faced with planning a funeral, there are many things to consider, but you are very emotionally drained, there are family wishes, and the financial burden.

Please take time to really think about everything, and do not be pressured into planning and paying for services that can send your family into bankruptcy.

1. Consider how you will feel now and in the future when you return to the place you have chosen to place your child's remains. It should be a place you will feel at peace returning to. For Desiree's brother & myself, we knew that she was a free spirit and would not want to be in a box, so we chose cremation and spread her ashes in the ocean.

2. Second, look into every option for services and burial. Do not let your emotional state allow you to purchase the funeral home's "package deal." This can cost more than of $20,000. Can you afford this cost?

3. Third, if you choose cremation, the Neptune Society is worth contacting for services. They specialize in ocean burials. You may also choose an urn or special box that you can keep at home instead of a burial, if that is what you wish to do.

"The best way to find yourself, is to lose yourself in the service of others."

~Mahatma Gandhi

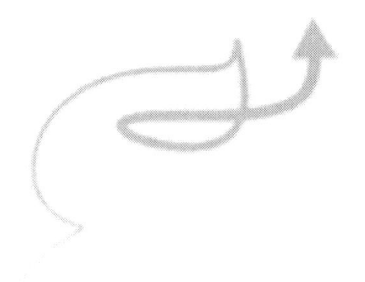

Chapter 8

Allow Yourself Time to Grieve and Heal

- ***Everyone's experience with death and grieving is different.***

    Only you know what is right for you. Do not allow anyone to tell you how you should be grieving and for how long. I am still grieving at times, even though it has been 26 years since my daughter went on to her next life.

- ***It's never something you "just get over."***

    If a friend or relative tells you that this is something you just "have to get over," they have never experienced the death of a child. This was my father's advice to me. You never just "get over it." The pain does soften in time - and it may take a long time. In the beginning, however, that is all you can think about. Try not to dwell on it too much. But the one thing you know is - you are forever changed, nothing is the same.

    Don't let the grief overcome you. Depression can be a killer, so if you sink into a depression that you cannot seem to recover from, please go see your doctor. Get some help and find a support group.

- ***Helping someone else can really help you.***

    Focusing on others in need or another parent that is also grieving can take you away from your own internal pain – even if just for a little while.

- ***Remember other members of the family are grieving too.***

    I did forget, and my son suffered for it. He was just 17-years-old and he felt so alone and was in so much pain. My daughter, Colleen, was 5-years-old, and it was so difficult to explain where her sister had gone and why she was not coming home. For the brothers and/or sisters, there are also support groups available.

- ***As a family, try to talk about each other's feelings.***

    If this is not possible for whatever reason, at least tell them you love them, and be there if they want to talk. If you find it hard to talk about your child, please find a good therapist (if you have not already done so). Otherwise there are many support groups available. Talking with others who are in the same situation as you is a great help for many reasons.

- ***Find comfort in helpful books.***

  I found a wonderful book written by Dr. Elizabeth Kubler-Ross called *Remember the Secret*. This book is a gentle way for children to learn about the value of life, as well as the reality of death & dying.

"It's not the goodbye that hurts, but it is the flashbacks that follow."

~The Notebook

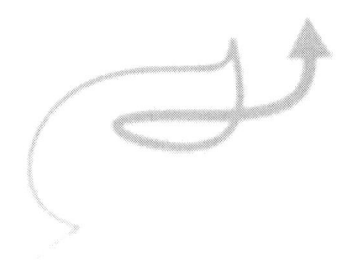

Chapter 9

Flashbacks – The Pain

- If you had a very painful experience with the loss of your child, it is not uncommon to have flashback memories of that experience, perhaps for years.

- ***These flashbacks can happen at any time, anywhere and can take you by complete surprise.***

  The suddenness can take your breath away. The emotional pain can stop you in your tracks. I once had a flashback as an ambulance passed by me with its siren and lights on. It triggered a full memory of the day they took my daughter away to the hospital, the day she passed away. I was driving and had to pull over, off the road. I started to cry and felt rather shaky. It took me a couple of minutes to let the flashback pass and regain my senses.

- ***It's OK - let yourself go with it, then BREATHE!***

  Tell yourself, *I am OK*. Wipe away the tears and say, *I love you up there and I miss you*. Try to go about your day the best you can.

  I still talk to my daughter, especially on her birthday when her sister & I put flowers in the ocean for her. Her brother paddles out on his surfboard in the bay where her ashes were spread and spends time with her, in a sense.

Believing that my child could somehow hear me gave me peace.

"As my sufferings mounted, I soon realized that there were two ways in which I could respond to my situation -- either to react with bitterness or seek to transform the suffering into a creative force. I decided to follow the latter course."

~Martin Luther King Jr.

Chapter 10

How to Save Your Own Sanity

- ***Even your belief in God can be shaken now.***

    If you have a favorite religious / spiritual counselor, make time to talk to them. All right, you do not have a belief in God, are your thoughts now, *"Why should I continue to live?"* If for no other reason, live for them.

- ***Do something nice for someone else in memory of your loved one.***

    Many church groups or local organizations that you may belong to know of a family in need or someone who has also had a recent death in their family. Bring a meal to the family or offer help in some way. Help an elder to mow their lawn, or go to the store for them - something as small as just talking to someone lonely can help you feel better.

- ***Don't stop enjoying life.***

    There are many old beliefs and customs surrounding death that are really not good for you mentally or physically. During these times of grief, it is thought that you should not be laughing or enjoying life. Do you believe that your child would want you to live your life to the fullest or sit around grieving? I believe they want the best for you. Even though it is very difficult in the beginning, take some time to enjoy yourself, either alone or with friends and family.

- ***You are always going to have memories, try to remember the good ones.***

And I hope and pray that you do not have a lot of regrets or "*I wish I would have*" thoughts, but only thoughts that you did everything you could to make your child's life a good one to the best of your ability and circumstances.

- ***Be gentle with yourself during holidays.***

Oh boy, surviving anniversaries and holidays are a challenge, to say the least. The anniversary of their passing is the worst. Christmas and their birthday are yet other times of anxiety and emotional pain. Plan on going somewhere special, away, if you can. Finding a new way of spending the holidays can really help you get through them.

- ***Avoid familiar and favorite places for a while.***

I recommend not going to your child's favorite places for a while, and stay away from big malls for shopping, especially during Christmas season. There are usually a lot of excited children and families in the mall, and I would get so anxious. Passing by my daughter's favorite jewelry store brought a lot of tears, I had to leave. It took many years to return to this store.

- ***Allow your holiday experience to be different.***

    If you are blessed to have other children, they can help you get through the holidays, but do not be surprised to find that you are not able to get very excited about decorating or having a family gatherings. Let the kids do the decorating and *find joy in their excitement.*

- ***Make your child's dream come true.***

    Finish a project or degree your loved one was working on; volunteer to help out with their favorite sports team; or work with disabled kids. It is so lifting to finish something your child felt passionate about, to fulfill their dream. My daughter was in college, working on a degree in Fashion Design and was not able to complete the degree. So I finished a Bachelor's degree and dedicated my graduation to her. Then I did something for myself and finished my Master's degree.

    There have been many stories in the news about parents starting a charity or foundation in their child's memory to help others. For these parents, their child lives on in doing this work.

- ***The pain of lost milestones.***

    Another time of emotional upset is when you start thinking of all the things in your child's life that you will not see - a graduation, going to prom, a wedding, grandchildren you will never have. Again, you can work through these times. Stop and *BREATHE*. If the tears start to flow, it is OK, you are OK. Our life continues regardless, and we have to try to make it the best life we can.

"Dance, when you're broken open. Dance, if you've torn the bandage off. Dance in the middle of fighting. Dance in your blood. Dance when you're perfectly free."

~Rumi

Chapter 11

Keep Living and Do What You Love.

- **Dance while you still can.**

    If you love to dance, take dance lessons or find a dance group that has regular weekly dances. Taking ballroom dance lessons was a lifesaver for me - mentally, physically, & emotionally. It is great exercise, and you cannot help laughing at yourself when you goof up like everyone else that is just beginning. And I found the love of my life through dancing!

- ***Sing it out!***

    Join a choir if you love to sing, maybe at your church or at the local community college.

- ***Express yourself through art.***

    Paint, draw, sculpt, create jewelry or other crafts. Start a garden of living plants such as herbs. They can be started anywhere, use a pot in a window or any tub if you do not have a yard.

- ***Volunteer*** – anywhere!

    Just a few to think about are:

    - ***The Humane Society*** - go walk the dogs

- Contact the **Salvation Army and Food Banks** - feed the homeless

- ***Meals-on-Wheels*** - feed the elderly

- ***Hospitals*** always need volunteers

- ***Charity Organizations or Foundations***

I find a lot of joy in volunteering and raising money for the *Make-A-Wish Foundation* and for the *Cystic Fibrosis Foundation.*

- **Lastly, *write a book or keep a journal.***

    Writing down your thoughts and feelings can be very healing, especially if you do not have someone to talk to who understands what you are going through, someone that has also experienced this kind of loss.

My last few words of encouragement:

Losing a loved one is never easy. It is very emotional and painful. But losing a child can be devastating on every level of your being. Personally, I have lost my only brother and both parents, but nothing compares to the loss of my daughter.

Continue to celebrate the life of your loved one even though you cannot see or touch them. Imagine their smile in your mind when something is done in their memory. Celebrate your other children if you have them. Life can be short; do not waste it - make wonderful memories.

I only hope I have helped a mother or father survive this complex and painful time in life. And just maybe you won't have to say, *Stop the world, I am getting off*.

Bless you all. Continue to live, love, laugh, and dance, in this moment, for you never know when your own life will come to an end.

Namaste!

Love to all,

Nancy

Resources:

Seattle Children's – seattlechildrens.org/clinics-programs

Healing Center – healingcenter.org

Swedish Medical Center – Bereavement & Support, has classes and resources

Hospice of Seattle – you can also find resources from Hospice Agencies around the country

Grief/Share Groups:

Compassionate Friends.org

Cancer Care, support for siblings – cancercare.org, childrenscause.org

Gold Star Moms – Military mother's group that supports other moms after their child has been killed in action.

Therapy:

Family support – www.archildren.org

American Association for Marriage & Family Therapy- *aamft.org*
National Hospice & Palliative Care – www.nhpco.org/pediatrics (see caring connections)

Summer Camps for Kids with special needs:

Camp resources – www.campresources.com, www.campforall.org, www.parentmap.com, look for friendship circle.

Always ask at the local Children's Hospital for resources like these above.

Ronald McDonald House (for lodging)

The hospital Social Worker also has information about lodging in your area.

Children's Medically Intensive Care Facilities

Seattle Areas:

Children's Country Home
14643 NE 166th St
Woodinville, WA 98072
425-806-9453

Ashley House Kids -
5 locations: Tacoma at Brown's Point, Enumclaw, Kent, Northshore, and Olympia

Bailey Boushay House
2720 E. Madison St
Seattle, WA 98112
206-322-5300

For in-home Private Duty Nursing through the Developmental Disabilities Administration (state of Washington):
Medically Intensive Children's Program (MICP) –
for children 17 years of age of younger
Contact: Doris Barret, RN, MBA

Nursing Services Unit Manager –
Doris.Barret@dshs.wa.gov
360-407-1504

Saif Hakim, Chief - Office of Residential, Employment, and Day Programs -
Saif.Hakim@dshs.wa.gov
360-407-1505

You can find Children's Medically Intensive Care Facilities in other States on the internet. Some examples are:
Caring Corner – Bakersfield, California
Angel View – Multiple locations; Coachella Valley and High Desert
Meza, Arizona – Bogden House
New York – Angela's House: multiple locations

Made in the USA
Columbia, SC
11 November 2017